HOW TO WRITE A SHORT PERSUASIVE ARGUMENT

A Step-by-Step Guide

Kelly J. Kirkland
©2013

For Sherrill Aberg (1924 – 2002)

INTRODUCTION

This is a guide to writing a short persuasive argument. Not an argument as in yelling and screaming, but an argument as in taking a position on an issue and defending it.

We will start from the beginning and move forward step-by-step. After a quick review of some basic principles, we will learn how to write a topic sentence; that is, a sentence that tells the reader what our position is on an issue. We will then learn how to write sentences that support the topic sentence. Next we will see how to put topic and supporting sentences together to form a paragraph and then how to organize paragraphs into an argument. Finally, we will talk about whether and how we want to deal with arguments that the other side might make to try to undermine yours.

We will learn by building a fun, light-hearted argument. But the techniques we will learn will let us write serious persuasive arguments for school, business, or anywhere else we need to write something to convince people that your opinion is correct.

A VERY QUICK REVIEW OF
SOME BASIC PRINCIPLES

Types of writing: There are a number of different types of writing. Some examples would be:

- narrative: "He wouldn't let me change lanes, so I put a curse on him and his children and his children's children."

- creative: "It was a dark and stormy night …."

- technical: "Be very careful that the two pieces of metal do not come into contact."

This book deals with yet another type, persuasive writing.

Parts of speech: There are already many books and online sources containing detailed information about grammar, including parts of speech. This is not another one. However, we do need to refresh our memories about four fundamental parts of speech: verbs, nouns, adverbs, and adjectives. Verbs or verb phrases are usually action words

3

or phrases; for example, "decide," "decided," "have decided," and "have been decided." However, some verbs or verb phrases express instead a state of being: "is," "was," "have been." Nouns are the names of things, either concrete things you can see, hear, taste, touch, or smell ("apple") or abstract things that you can't ("privilege"). Many abstract nouns are built from verbs ("decision"). Adverbs modify verbs or verb phrases ("decided wisely"), and adjectives modify nouns ("wise decision").

Active vs. passive voice: Verbs can appear in either the active or passive voice. A sentence written in the active voice usually takes the form: the actor – the action – the object of the action: "I hit the ball." A sentence written in the passive voice usually takes the form: the object of the action – the action – the actor: "The ball was hit by me."

Punctuation and spelling: Again, there are already many books and online sources containing information about punctuation and spelling. You simply must use proper punctuation and spelling in any kind of writing—especially in persuasive writing, where sloppy punctuation and incorrect spelling may signal the reader that you are not a careful person and that your lack of care may carry over to the substance of your argument. Always proofread everything you write, starting with the last paragraph and working your way to the first.

HOW TO WRITE A GOOD SENTENCE

The best way to learn how to write a good sentence is to start with a bad one and change it to a good one. Let's start with this one:

> I believe that a timely evacuation of Earth should be done by mankind.

Why is this sentence poorly written? First, the sentence isn't really about you; you're not trying to convince people to do something to or about you. Let's delete from the sentence the phrase "I believe that."

Rule 1: Leave out phrases like "I believe," "I think," "I suppose," and the like. Just say what you want to say.

The sentence now reads:

A timely evacuation of the Earth should be done by mankind.

That still needs work, so let's dig a little deeper. What is the verb phrase in this sentence? "Should be done." But what action are we really talking about in this sentence? Evacuating Earth. We have turned the real verb— "evacuate"—into a noun—"evacuation." When you turn a strong action verb into a noun and replace it with a weak verb (often some form of the verb "to be" or "to do"), you weaken the entire sentence.

Rule 2: Use strong verbs; don't turn them into nouns and replace them with weak verbs.

We can rewrite the sentence to read:

Earth should be evacuated in a timely manner
by mankind.

That's better, but let's keep going. Do we really need the adverbial phrase "in a timely manner"? Think about it—would anyone really argue in favor of evacuating the Earth in an untimely manner?

Rule 3: Use adverbs, adverbial phrases, adjectives, and adjectival phrases only when they are really necessary.

So now the sentence reads:

Earth should be evacuated by mankind.

The verb phrase is "should be evacuated," but who should evacuate? Mankind. There may be times when you want to de-emphasize who is doing the action—"The keys were lost by me" rather than "I lost the keys." But generally you want to write in the active voice.

Rule 4: Unless you want to de-emphasize who did something, write in the active voice.

We can therefore restate the sentence:

Mankind should evacuate Earth.

That's pretty good, but when you talk to your family or friends, do you often use the word "evacuate"? This sentence sounds like police officers sometimes do when they testify in court:

Q: "When you got to the scene, officer, what did you do?"

A: "I exited my vehicle."

Q: "Do you mean that you got out of your car?"

A: "Um … yes."

If you don't go around saying fancy words like "evacuate," don't use them when you write. Use a more common word like "leave."

Rule 5: Use the simplest words that accurately say what you want to say.

We started with this sentence:

I believe that a timely evacuation of Earth should be done by mankind.

We now have this one:

Mankind should leave Earth.

That is a good, strong sentence. We can call this our "topic sentence"; it sets out the position we want to defend. We can build solid arguments with sentences like this one.

Remember—to write a strong sentence:

Leave yourself out of it.

Use strong action verbs.

Use adverbs, adverbial phrases, adjectives, and adjectival phrases sparingly.

Use the active voice.

Use simple words.

HOW TO WRITE A GOOD SUPPORTING SENTENCE

Let's start where we left off:

Mankind should leave Earth.

If you write an argument that starts with this sentence, and you are certain that every single one of your readers agrees with you, you can stop right there. You have made your point.

But usually you are not certain whether everyone agrees with you or you know that they do not. You then need to support your opinion. Assuming that each of them is true, which of these four sentences best supports an opinion that mankind should leave Earth?

1.   Earth turns on its axis once every 24 hours.

2.   Earth looks blue from space.

3.   Living on Earth is holding us back.

4.   Titanium is pretty strong stuff.

You can probably use common sense to figure out that the third sentence provides the most support for the sentence "Mankind should leave Earth."

But let's try to tease out exactly why common sense leads us to that conclusion. We are interested in whether the supporting sentence—assuming it is true—gives us a good reason to believe that the topic sentence is true. A useful way to test this is to use the "Because Test."

The Because Test is simple. Write the topic sentence (minus the period); then write the word "because"; then write the supporting sentence (without capitalizing the first word). Thus:

1.   Mankind should leave Earth because Earth turns on its axis once every 24 hours.

2.   Mankind should leave Earth because Earth looks blue from space.

3.   Mankind should leave Earth because living on Earth is holding us back.

4.   Mankind should leave Earth because titanium is pretty strong stuff.

When you push the two sentences together so that they are separated only by the word "because," it becomes easier to see if there is a strong logical connection between the two. In this case, the third sentence "makes the most sense" because the logical connection between the two parts is much stronger than it is for any of the other sentences. In other words, the fact that living on Earth is holding us back—if true—is indeed a good reason for believing that mankind should leave Earth. Therefore, the sentence "Living on Earth is holding us back" is a good supporting sentence for the sentence "Mankind should leave Earth."

At this point we need to take a little detour to consider a small problem that comes up sometimes when we try to apply the Because Test. Take a look at this paragraph:

Mankind should leave Earth. I conducted a survey of people around the world. I asked 1,000 people from each country if they liked living on Earth. Almost 80% of them said that they were tired of living on Earth and would rather live somewhere else.

It has the same topic sentence as the one we have been considering—"Mankind should leave Earth." Following that topic sentence are three sentences that, considered together, provide good support for the first sentence. But watch what happens when we apply the Because Test to one of them by itself:

> Mankind should leave Earth because I conducted a survey of people from around the world.

By itself, that one sentence fails the Because Test.

When we apply the Because Test, therefore, we must sometimes combine two or more sentences into one:

> Mankind should leave Earth because I conducted a survey of people around the world and I asked 1,000 people from each

country if they liked living on Earth and almost 80% of them said that they were tired of living on Earth and would rather live somewhere.

This makes sense, even if it is clearly a run-on sentence. Remember that we run these sentences together only in order to apply the Because Test. If they pass the Because Test and we decide to put them in our argument, we restore them as separate sentences:

Mankind should leave Earth. I conducted a survey of people around the world. I asked 1,000 people from each country if they liked living on Earth. Almost 80% of them said that they were tired of living on Earth and would rather live somewhere else.

The key point is that sometimes we take separate sentences and run them together into one sentence solely to see if together they pass the Because Test.

Another detour: Sometimes we need to replace the Because Test with the For Example Test. To do that we connect the two sentences by writing the first sentence without the period; add a semi-colon (;); add the words "for example" followed by a comma; and then write the second sentence (without capitalizing the first word).

Let's see how this works. For just a moment, suppose we change our topic sentence to read:

There are several reasons why mankind should leave Earth.

If we try to support that sentence with the sentence "Earth has a lot of hurricanes," and then apply the Because Test, we get:

There are several reasons why mankind should leave Earth because Earth has a lot of hurricanes.

That doesn't make any sense, and therefore this supporting sentence fails the Because Test.

But wait! The For Example Test gives us:

There are several reasons why mankind should leave Earth; for example, Earth has a lot of hurricanes.

That works just fine and tells us that the second sentence is a good supporting sentence for the first. So the For Example Test can fill in for the Because Test.

One last point: you should ignore introductory "filler" words or phrases such as "finally" or "in addition" when applying the Because Test or the For Example Test. These words and phrases make the paragraph sound better but add nothing to the substance of the paragraph. They play no role in the Because Test and the For Example Test.

As we shall see, the Because Test and the For Example Test are the keys to writing a persuasive argument. You will usually use the Because Test: (i) write the topic sentence without the period; (ii) add the word "because"; and (iii) then write the supporting sentence without capitalizing the first word. If the resulting sentence makes sense, you know you have a good supporting sentence.

HOW TO WRITE A GOOD PARAGRAPH

Once we know how to write a good topic sentence and a good supporting sentence, it is easy to write a good paragraph. A good paragraph consists of (i) a good topic sentence, (ii) two to four good supporting sentences, and (iii) a good concluding sentence.

Let's go back to where we were before we took those detours. So far we have:

Mankind should leave Earth. Living on Earth is holding us back.

We need a few more good supporting sentences. Let's add two more, for a total of three:

Staying on Earth is impractical.

Finally, Earth is boring.

22

To make sure these are good supporting sentences, we apply the Because Test:

Mankind should leave Earth because staying on Earth is impractical.

Mankind should leave Earth because Earth is boring.

Both of these sentences (if true) make sense, so we know we have two good supporting sentences.

We now add a good concluding sentence. To do that, we just restate the topic sentence; that is, we say the same thing in different words. Perhaps something like:

It is time for us to leave.

Our paragraph therefore reads:

> Mankind should leave Earth. Living on Earth is holding us back. Staying on Earth is impractical. Finally, Earth is boring. It is time for us to leave.

That is a perfectly good paragraph and a great way to start our argument.

HOW TO WRITE A GOOD ARGUMENT

Once again, let's start where we left off:

Mankind should leave Earth. Living on Earth is holding us back. Staying here is impractical. Finally, Earth is boring. It is time for us to leave.

Now let's give each sentence an identifying letter—T stands for the topic sentence; X, Y, and Z are the supporting sentences; and C is the concluding sentence:

T: Mankind should leave Earth.

X: Living on Earth is holding us back.

Y: Staying here is impractical.

Z: Finally, Earth is boring.

C: It is time for us to leave.

To make sure we understand what we're doing here, let's rewrite our paragraph with the appropriate letter in brackets before each sentence:

[T] Mankind should leave Earth. [X] Living on Earth is holding us back. [Y] Staying here is impractical. [Z] Finally, Earth is boring. [C] It is time for us to leave.

Of course, we don't include the bracketed letters in the final version of our argument. They're in there only temporarily to help us understand what's coming next.

We need to go through this next part very carefully. We are now ready to outline the rest of the argument. The following outline may look very complicated at first, but once you understand what it means, you can actually plug sentences into it to write a persuasive argument very quickly. Let's first just take a quick look at the whole outline:

First Paragraph

T

X

Y

Z

C

Second Paragraph

x

x_1

x_2

x_3

x_r

Third Paragraph

y

y_1

y_2

y_3

y_r

Fourth Paragraph

z

z_1

z_2

z_3

z_r

Fifth Paragraph

T_r

C_r

Let's see what we have done—it's not as complicated as it first appears. We already know what sentence X is: "Living on Earth is holding us back." We build the second paragraph by simply taking the first supporting sentence from the first paragraph—that is, sentence X—and making it the topic sentence of the second paragraph. We will probably change the wording slightly because it will sound a little silly if we repeat it word-for-word, maybe something like:

[x]   Living on Earth is starting to cause us problems.

In our outline, we call this sentence "x." The small "x" reminds us that this sentence is simply another version of sentence "X" from our first paragraph.

We then write three (actually, anywhere from two to four) supporting sentences for this new topic sentence using the Because Test or the For Example Test. In the outline, the little numbers below and to the right of a letter mean that these are supporting sentences. Thus, x_1, x_2, and x_3 are supporting sentences for sentence x (which once again is sentence X from our first paragraph as we have rewritten it). Similarly, y_1, y_2, and y_3 are supporting sentences for sentence y (which is sentence Y as we have rewritten it), and z_1, z_2, and z_3 are supporting sentences for sentence z (which is sentence Z as we have rewritten it).

Let's write three supporting sentences for sentence x ("Living on Earth is starting to cause us problems."):

[x_1]   Hurricanes are killing people and destroying a lot of the neat stuff we have built.

[x_2]   Earthquakes are even worse.

[x_3]   Climate change could actually wipe us out.

Finally, we repeat the topic sentence (sentence x), changing the wording again but keeping the same meaning:

Earth is beginning to be a difficult place to live.

We'll call this sentence "x_r" because it is the rewritten version of sentence x (which itself is a rewritten version of sentence X). The rewriting process is therefore: $X \rightarrow x \rightarrow x_r$.

We end up with this for our second paragraph:

[x] Living on Earth is starting to cause us problems. [x_1] Hurricanes are killing people and destroying a lot of the neat stuff we have built. [x_2] Earthquakes are even worse. [x_3] Climate change could actually wipe us out. [xr] Earth is beginning to be a difficult place to live.

We can build a third and fourth paragraph the same way:

[y] Staying here is impractical. [y_1] For example, oceans cover most of the Earth's surface and we can't live on or under the ocean for long. [y_2] In addition, a lot of the dry land is desert or covered by ice. [y_r] It is simply ridiculous for us to live on a planet where most of the surface is useless.

[z] Let's face it—it's boring here. [z_1] We have seen everything there is to see on Earth. [z_2] Writers and poets have said everything there is to say about living here. [z_3] We can't even be bothered to get up early just to watch the sunrise. [z_r] Yawn!

Finally, writing the concluding paragraph to the argument takes a little practice. Basically we need at least two sentences. The idea is not to add anything new when we are wrapping up but rather to restate our main point in a slightly different way than we phrased it earlier. Maybe something like this:

$[T_r]$ Let's get out of here. $[C_r]$ There must be better planets out there.

We'll call these sentences T_r and C_r because they are the rewritten versions of sentences T and C in our first paragraph.

Notice that the total number of paragraphs in the argument depends upon how many supporting sentences we put in the first paragraph. If there are two supporting sentences, there will be four paragraphs in all. Using three supporting sentences in the first paragraph gives us a total of five paragraphs, which is what this outline shows. Using four supporting sentences gives us six paragraphs. Go back to the outline and make sure that you understand how that works.

Let's see what the whole argument looks like:

Mankind should leave Earth. Living on Earth is holding us back. Staying here is impractical. Finally, Earth is boring. It is time for us to leave.

Living on Earth is starting to cause us problems. Hurricanes are killing people and destroying a lot of the neat stuff we have built. Earthquakes are even worse. Climate change could actually wipe us out. Earth is beginning to be a difficult place to live.

Staying here is impractical. For example, oceans cover most of the Earth's surface and we can't live on or under the ocean for long. In addition, a lot of the dry land is desert or covered by ice. It is simply ridiculous for us to live on a planet where most of the surface is useless.

Let's face it—it's boring here. We have seen everything there is to see on Earth. Writers and poets have said everything there is to say about living here. We can't even be bothered to get up early just to look at the sunrise. Yawn!

Let's get out of here. There must be better planets out there.

Notice three things about this argument. First, it is important that the supporting sentences in the first paragraph be general enough that they can serve as the topic sentences for the following paragraphs. You may have to experiment a little. A sentence such as "There are seventeen computers on the fourth floor" doesn't leave you anywhere to go when you use it as a topic sentence for a later paragraph.

Second, some of the supporting sentences in the third and fourth paragraphs use the For Example Test. We have even used the phrase "for example" in one of the supporting sentences. Sometimes a good supporting sentence will pass both tests, but as long as your supporting sentence passes either test, you are fine.

Third, the third paragraph has two supporting sentences, not three. You may want to make three supporting sentences per paragraph the usual way to write a paragraph but give yourself permission to change to two or four supporting sentences where necessary or appropriate.

Our sample argument is not exactly the stuff for which they award the Nobel Prize for Literature. But it is a perfectly good, well-organized argument that makes its point and then adds sentences that support that point. The Because Test (or the For Example Test) makes sure of that.

ANOTHER EXAMPLE

That argument was more than a little tongue-in-cheek. Let's take a look at a more serious example of a short persuasive argument:

First Paragraph

T: Our company should open stores in Canada.

X: The market for our products in Canada is very similar to the market for our products in the United States.

Y: We can use all of our current advertising.

Z: There are many tech savvy sales people in Canada.

C: Opening an office in Canada makes sense.

Second Paragraph

x: There are no significant differences between the markets for our products in the two countries.

x_1:   Both the United States and Canada have a lot of people who can afford to spend $100 to $200 for our products.

x_2:   Both countries have many shopping malls, which is where our stores are usually located.

x_3:   Finally, Canadians are just as interested in high tech gadgets as Americans are.

x_r: Our products will fit easily into the Canadian market.

Third Paragraph

y: Our current advertising works just as well in Canada as it does in the United States.

y_1: For example, nothing in our TV ad is specific to the United States.

y_2: With small changes in spelling, the same is true with our print ads.

y_3: Our Internet ads are already available to any Canadian with access to the Internet.

y_r: Additional advertising costs to enter the Canadian market should be minimal.

Fourth Paragraph

z: It should not be difficult to find tech savvy sales people in Canada.

z_1:   Technological know-how is widespread in Canada, particularly among younger people

z_2:   Many Canadians would view a job with our company as highly desirable.

z_r: It should be relatively easy to staff new stores in Canada.

Fifth Paragraph

T_r: Our company should expand into Canada.

C_r: It is the logical next frontier.

42

Or in normal paragraph form:

Our company should open stores in Canada. The market for our products in Canada is very similar to the market for our products in the United States. We can use all of our current advertising. There are many tech savvy sales people in Canada. Opening an office in Canada makes sense.

There are no significant differences between the markets for our products in the two countries. Both the United States and Canada have a lot of people who can afford to spend $100 to $200 for our products. Both countries have many shopping malls, which is where our stores are usually located. Finally, Canadians are just as interested in high tech gadgets as Americans are. Our products will fit easily into the Canadian market.

Our current advertising works just as well in Canada as it does in the United States. For example, nothing in our TV ad is specific to the United States. With small changes in spelling, the same is true with our print ads. Our Internet ads are already available to any Canadian with access to the Internet. Additional advertising costs to enter the Canadian market should be minimal.

It should not be difficult to find tech savvy sales people in Canada. Technological know-how is widespread in Canada, particularly among younger people. Many

Canadians would view a job with our company as highly desirable. It should be relatively easy to staff new stores in Canada.

Our company should expand into Canada. It is the logical next frontier.

ADDRESSING THE OTHER SIDE'S ARGUMENTS

We've just written a good argument that supports your opinion that your company should open stores in Canada. Of course, there are probably also good reasons why it shouldn't. It is rare that your opinion is the only reasonable opinion—and if you think that it is, you probably need to think about the whole issue some more.

In the Middle Ages scholars followed very strict rules when they debated. Most of those rules are inapplicable to life in the 21st Century. But there is one that we need to resurrect and reintroduce into modern life.

In medieval universities it was customary to first state the proposition that you were going to defend: let's call it "P". You then said, "Vedetur quod non [P] ...." [In medieval Latin it is pronounced roughly "VAY duh toor kwode NAWN.] It means, "It seems that not [P]," as in "It seems that P is not true."

What followed—and this is the key point—were a few of the very best arguments that the scholar could think of against the position he was defending. It was a matter of honor, and the mark of a truly good scholar, to think up even better arguments than his opponent had come up with. Having done that, a good scholar proceeded to refute each of these counter-arguments to his position. Refuting the strongest arguments he could think of against T was a critical part of the whole exercise of defending T.

The ethics of debate have deteriorated greatly since medieval times. Today talking heads on TV usually deal with opponents by talking louder and faster than they do or simply by calling them "idiots" or worse. A strong dose of "vedetur quod non" would do us good today.

Thus, after setting out the arguments in favor of your position as we learned earlier, consider stating and refuting the best arguments against your position. It is not essential that you do this, but if you do, you will gain a well-deserved and precious reputation as a fair-minded person, someone who should be listened to.

Specifically, what you should do is write that the best arguments against your position are A and B. Then write a paragraph refuting each argument, that is, A is weak (or false) due to A_1, A_2, and A_3; and B is also weak due to B_1, B_2, and B_3. As always, use the Because Test or the For Example Test.

You will probably want to do this after you have presented your own position. Maybe something like this:

First Paragraph

T

X

Y

Z

C

Second Paragraph

x

x_1

x_2

x_3

x_r

Third Paragraph

y

y_1

y_2

y_3

y_r

Fourth Paragraph

z

z_1

z_2

z_3

z_r

Fifth Paragraph

The two best arguments against T are A and B.

Neither of these arguments is strong, however.

Sixth Paragraph

A is weak (or false).

A_1

A_2

A_3

A is weak (rewritten).

Seventh Paragraph

B is also weak (or false).

B_1

B_2

B_3

B is weak (rewritten)

Eighth Paragraph

T_r

C_r

Refuting the best counterarguments to your position is a powerful tool for persuading your readers that you are right. It also makes you think through the whole topic to make sure you are comfortable with your own position.

CONCLUSION

Learning how to write a short persuasive argument is a useful and powerful skill. Like all skills, it gets easier with practice. So ... start writing!